Love'em
Lead'em

Inspiration And Encouragement
For Educators.

Love'em and Lead'em
Inspiration and Encouragement for Educators

Love'em And Lead'em

Inspiration And Encouragement
For Educators.

You are a blessing!

Love'em and Lead'em,

Scott Barron

BY

SCOTT E. BARRON

This book is dedicated to the many educators who have been an inspiration in my life, especially Tammy Barron, Sue Barron, Ed Barron, and Carroll Sue Priddy. You changed my life, and I love teaching and learning because of you.

CONTENTS

INTRODUCTION

Thank you for your commitment as a talented, energized, engaged educator.

Whether you are an administrator, teacher, coach, staff member, board member, parent, minister, or just love to teach, this book was written specifically for you. These messages of encouragement are for anyone and everyone involved in education at all levels of schooling: preschool, K-12, higher ed, vocational, professional, and others.

As Educators, we change lives, change society, and even change the world!

We impart knowledge and inspire thinking.
We deliver both formal and informal instruction combined with practical wisdom and a love for Truth.
We invest in our students, whether appreciated or not, creatively and persistently overcoming the barriers to growth.

The world needs more gifted educators throughout all genres of education while also retaining those who have committed to this noble profession.

Love' em and Lead em: Inspiration and Encouragement for Educators was written to encourage and elevate those who educate, with gratitude for the work and a call to lead forward with courage and strength.

A school is a fragile ecosystem of relationships that requires an unusually strong capacity for love, grace, and forgiveness.

In the current climate, educators are tired—tired of the conflict, confusion, distractions, and stress. As a result, educational institutions are finding it harder and harder to sustain their people—meanwhile the school year is unrelenting in its deadlines and pace.

Respect for educators continues to wane as the court of public opinion, expressed in social media and other platforms, questions the integrity and acumen of the very people who seek to serve them.

All school employees feel the weight of these pressures.

This book is a collection of inspirational messages that can be read as a daily or weekly reflection. Educators have a unique vernacular that is used throughout this book, connecting with them at a deeper level in the context of their world. Each chapter may be used for personal reflection or as a conversation starter for professional development and important dialogue to build culture.

These messages were originally shared in a weekly email to thousands of educators around the world who responded with great appreciation for the understanding and wisdom expressed. Below are some sample email responses we received.

"I thought this was a great message and one that definitely resonated with me. Thanks!"
— Scott S., Director of School Operations

"Awesome message! Thank you so much for the uplifting support."
— Jocelyn P., School Director

"You couldn't have said it better. We forwarded this to our entire network of school leaders. Thank you for the affirming encouragement!"
— Valerie B., Superintendent

"I love receiving your weekly messages of encouragement for educators. Sometimes it feels like you're reading my mind. Your ministry matters."
— Rob R., Head of School

Most people hope to be remembered by someone. Educators are remembered by hundreds and thousands because of their multigenerational influence.

Thank you for your service as an educator!

In light of the hectic pace of the school schedule and calendar, we have to be careful to slow down to the pace of life so that grace and truth are sustained.

By habitually allowing time for contemplation, prayer, and study, we enable our heart, mind, and soul to be prepared and properly renewed for this commitment.

You were created for a purpose, my friend, and my hope is that you experience a little more joy and appreciation through this book.

To subscribe to the Weekly Encouragement for Educators email, visit www.EdFellowship.org

SOMETHING BIGGER

*It is easier to build strong children
than to repair broken men.*

—FREDERICK DOUGLASS

We have the privilege of visiting many educators each year. When we walk into a school for the first time, we quickly begin to get a sense of the people and their relationships with one another by the verbal and non-verbal language.

Fresh eyes help us all get past our own confirmation bias and more accurately understand what it's like to come into our environment and be around our school.

As leaders, we set the tone for the culture, which is a vital part of our contribution. We want to set a tone that inspires trust, encouraging honest communication and maximum engagement.

*We build too many walls
and not enough bridges.*
—Isaac Newton

Teachers, staff, students, and parents all need us to remind them that they are valuable and valued. We can't let them forget that!

So, we build them up and remind them that they're important and loved. It only takes one person to have faith in another, to care and build them up.
We carefully choose our words and demonstrate real love through our actions, enabling us to be happier and our school to be a place where human beings thrive.

It's important that we look at each constituency in our school as distinct and then find ways to serve them to the best of our abilities.

Gracious words are a honeycomb,
sweet to the soul and healing to the bones.
— Proverbs 16:24

Children and adults look up to us, so we have a responsibility in how we treat and respect them.

There are so many other people in this world who try to make them feel inadequate.

Address them by name and remember their interests.

Know them: their dreams, goals, and love language.

Respect them out of authentic humility.

Celebrate them, recognizing their progress and achievements.

Believe in them, assuming the best and encouraging greatness.

Value them, seeking their advice and wisdom.

Trust them with the data and the truth.

Make a difference as a life builder, my friend, enabling the joy and success of those in your sphere of influence.

Love'em and Lead'em!

Active Question

Did I do my best to lead bigger today?

WE DO HARD THINGS

We do these things,
not because they are easy,
but because they are hard.

—JOHN F. KENNEDY

President John F. Kennedy's address in 1962 inspired support for America's mission to be the first country to land on the moon before the end of the decade.

At the time, scientists didn't have the knowledge, the materials, or the tools to accomplish this "far out" goal--especially in just seven years.

He understood that the path to excellence cannot be walked alone and is achieved only by an insatiable drive to win. So he appealed to the nation to come together for a remarkable challenge:

> *One that we are willing to accept,*
> *one we are unwilling to postpone,*
> *and one which we intend to win.*

As educators today, we face circumstances that feel overwhelming.

But we know that leadership and growth happen only through courageous vision and perseverance through hard times and hard things.

We refuse to cower to the disparagement and dysfunction that relentlessly seek to discourage us.

Managing through a pandemic is hard.
Conflict over policies and mandates is hard.
Making wise decisions while also maintaining vital relationships is hard.
Educating children and parents is hard.
Loving educators and families through all of this is hard.

> *Do not follow where the path may lead.*
> *Go instead where there is no path and leave a trail.*
> —Ralph Waldo Emerson

And that's why we're educators.

We are educators, not because it's easy, but because it's hard!

We have the courage and the determination to inspire our faculty to unity in purpose and a culture of deep trust.

We are thick-skinned while also remaining sensitive to the needs of our people and sustaining a willingness to listen.

Where there is no vision,
the people perish.
—Proverbs 29:18

As our collective commitment to the mission and to each other grows, so does our impact and success. The roots of our relationships go deeper, giving us a powerful advantage in the battle for the hearts and minds of our people.

Love'em and Lead'em!

Active Question

Did I do my best to do the hard things today?

CLEAR DIRECTION

If one advances confidently in the direction of his dreams, and endeavors to live the life, which he has imagined, he will meet with a success unexpected in common hours.

— HENRY DAVID THOREAU

When driving around a major city or to somewhere new, we're very thankful for phone apps that provide turn-by-turn directions--they (usually) take the mystery out of how to get where we want to go and help us get there on the fastest route.

Knowing where we're going is especially important when leading a caravan of others. I remember once when several cars were following me to a school event, and I missed a critical turn. It was quite embarrassing having to make that next U-turn with all those people following.

They didn't let me forget that moment for a while!

The drivers in that long line were counting on me to get them to our destination, but I looked lost. Not a good way to build confidence in my leadership.

It's even worse in those bigger moments of life when we lack direction.

How do we find our course...

> *...to get where we want to go in life?*
> *...to create a vision and plan for our organization?*

We have to know where we're going if we expect others to join us on the journey of growing up and elevating performance.

Everyone needs to understand how their work contributes to the larger goals and plans. They need to feel valued and remember that they're part of something more than just their individual role.

> *The best way to lengthen out our days is to walk*
> *steadily and with a purpose.*
> — Charles Dickens

Providing clear direction is part of our commitment to lead and love.

It's hard to be motivated when there is a sense of confusion and uncertainty, so we have to plan in order to lead with a clear sense of purpose.

Vagueness is a major contributor to disfunction. Regardless of tenure or age, that means starting by communicating clear and aspirational expectations. Then following up and following through with consistent discipline.

Effective educators set the pace by ensuring expectations are translated into day-to-day habits to foster a culture of cohesiveness, consistency, and growth.

Live with clarity, staying on track to your goals.

Love'em and Lead'em!

> # Active Question
>
> *Did I do my best to pursue my dreams today?*

CHANGE AGENT

In times of change, learners inherit the Earth while the learned find themselves beautifully equipped to deal with a world that no longer exists.

— ERIC HOFFER

Do you think of yourself as a change agent?

A change agent is a catalyst who makes things happen through a coordinated effort to create a better future. They often play the role of a coach, counselor, or teacher, providing the pathway to new ways of thinking and being.

They champion change and growth, helping overcome inevitable areas of resistance.

They guide colleagues through the journey to build trust and active participation.

They embrace and give feedback to increase wisdom and better decisions.

Sound familiar?

Yes, my friend, as an educator, you are a change agent!

It may be hard for an egg
to turn into a bird:
It would be a jolly sight
harder for it to learn to
fly while remaining an egg.
— C. S. Lewis

Powerful forces have changed our world, especially over the last few years, sadly altering the experience of childhood for many students.

Fulfilling our calling to this work requires adapting to these realities, or else we'll find ourselves futilely pushing back against a tide that will ultimately overwhelm.

Flexibility is a sign of intelligence and is fundamental to our effectiveness.

We must not underestimate our capacity to purposefully change, sustaining an attitude that is open to new ideas with a willingness to learn and grow.

I alone cannot change the world,
but I can cast a stone across the waters
to create many ripples.
— Mother Teresa

We are change agents who are never satisfied with mediocrity or a fixed mindset.
We resist the temptation of overvaluing what is as compared to what could be.

Such fear-based thinking stifles the energy and engagement of our people.

Change is seldom pain-free and almost always includes drawbacks and consequences, but that's how we grow to be our best.

Our success is determined by our ability to learn and adapt faster and more effectively with an authentic love for this work and for each other.

Stay hungry and curious, constantly ready to fulfill your role as a change agent that enables the pathway to excellence.

Love'em and Lead'em!

Active Question

Did I do my best to be a purposeful change agent today?

WHO ARE YOU?

*My failures may be my greatest
successes. It is in failure that I have
often drawn closer to God, learn to
depend more on Him than myself,
gained self-knowledge, and seen
things in their right perspective.*

— MOTHER ANGELICA

Who are you?

That is perhaps the most important question each one of us,
and especially every educator has to authentically answer.

Who are you?
I really wanna know.
I really wanna know.
Come on, tell me, who are you, you, you, you?
Who are you?
Who are you?

These lyrics by *The Who* serve as a point of reflection and a call
to action.

> *The purposes of a person's heart are deep waters, but one who has insight draws them out.*
> — Proverbs 20:5

In our research on The Key Intelligences of Highly Effective Educators, self-awareness is by far and away the top attribute identified.

Knowing ourselves is a journey that accurately reveals who we are as human beings: Our talents, our strengths, our natural instincts, our learned habits, our behavioral triggers, etc.

Most stop short on self-discovery because it requires hard work and vulnerability, bringing us face-to-face with how we're living our lives and whether or not we're in alignment with our stated beliefs and purpose.

Some people live their entire existence never truly defining their purpose. They never know, because they never ask and then truly seek.

Discovering our purpose can be one of the most powerful experiences of understanding who we are and would be a remarkable addition to a professional growth plan.

> *Life is never made unbearable by circumstances,*
> *but only by lack of meaning and purpose.*
> – Viktor Frankl

Who?

That's our question as we enter into a new season of opportunities, challenges, and living.

Who am I?
Who influences me?
Who do I serve?
Who is on my team?

Consider keeping a journal of your self-discovery. Such a journal works for people and for organizations. Honesty and intentionality about the answers to these questions form the foundation of a purpose-driven life and legacy.

Love'em and Lead'em!

Active Question

Did I do my best to be who I want to be today?

GREAT MEMORIES

*No memory is ever alone; it's at
the end of a trail of memories,
a dozen trails that each have
their own associations.*

— LOUIS L'AMOUR

Once the family left after the holidays, we had lots of cleaning up to do.

Floors, counters, laundry, dishes, trash cans, …all had to be cleaned and order restored.

Evidence of our time together could be found everywhere:

toothbrush, sock, cups, small fingerprints across the windows, misplaced remote control, drink stains, score pad from the card games, and the list goes on.

All of these are part of the joy of celebrating together and making special memories.

We all have our time machines. Some take us back, they're called memories. Some take us forward, they're called dreams.
— Jeremy Irons

The most beautiful things in life are those special moments and memories—If we don't celebrate those, they just pass us by, leaving us less fulfilled.

What are the memories we're making together as educators? How will we create even better experiences the rest of this year? We can create a clear pathway to success for others to follow. We can lead a healthy, beautiful organization that inspires educators and students.
We can enable authentic excellence that obliterates dysfunctional silos and distrust.

Because of our calling, we choose to remember the best about people and gracefully release them from errors and sins of yesterday.

> *I've always been fascinated by*
> *memory and dreams because*
> *they are both completely our own.*
> *No one else has the same memories.*
> *No one has the same dreams.*
> — Lois Lowry

Memories are powerful, but it's our vision that elevates and energizes people.

We give hope and enable dreams through education.

Our distinctive is being passionate and persistent about this work, with the intelligence and experience to create real life change. Wow!

So many great memories will be made because of our uncon-ditional, tireless love.

Make some powerful memories—the kind that inspire new dreams.

Love'em and Lead'em!

Active Question

Did I do my best to create great memories and inspire dreams today?

ERUPTIONS HAPPEN

Every morning I jump out of bed and step on a landmine. The landmine is me. After the explosion, I spend the rest of the day putting the pieces together.

— RAY BRADBURY

In 2021, an undersea volcano erupted near Tonga out in the Pacific Ocean.

Have you seen the satellite images that show the monumental explosion?

The data from the event provided incredible insight about how massive and historic it was.

(even more epic than Eddie Van Halen's Eruption—if you know, you know)

It was bigger than the largest nuclear detonation ever conducted previously!

It was not only a once-in-a-lifetime event—it was quite literally a once-in-a-millennium event because it takes about 1,000 years for that much magma to build up and reach the boiling point.

Wars spring from unseen and generally insignificant causes,
the first outbreak being often but an explosion of anger.
— Thucydides

As educators, we encounter eruptions—of ideas, understanding, frustration, etc.

The first two are exciting because they are the fulfillment of our purpose.

Eruptions of frustration, however, are certainly less desirable because they are usually rooted in us under-delivering on their expectations, combined with insufficient communication and delayed response.

That's a recipe for conflict and dysfunction, which brings out our worst prejudices.

How pitiful a sight is a man who is strong in many ways
but who loses all control of himself when some little thing,
usually of no significant consequence, disturbs his equanimity.
— Gordon B. Hinckley

We're less likely to be prejudiced against people we know than those we don't.

Our human tendency is to make negative assumptions with imagined narratives and stereotypes about their motivations and beliefs. That gives fuel to gossip and dissension that undermines our desired culture of trust and belonging.

If we take the time to get to know them, though, negative assumptions are often replaced with deeper knowledge that enables us to take the steps to strengthen relationships.

Wisely manage the inevitable eruptions, my friend, taking the time to celebrate growth and wisely seeking to understand what's behind expressions of frustration because you genuinely care.

Love'em and Lead'em!

Active Question

Did I make time to respond to the eruptions as a peacemaker today?

RAISED TO THE POWER OF TEAM

No matter how brilliant your mind or strategy,
if you're playing a solo game,
you'll always lose out to a team.

– REID HOFFMAN

The challenges for educators are plentiful and growing and are generally underestimated by parents, policymakers, and pundits.

You've been doing this long enough to know that we will have lots of opportunities to get distracted and discouraged as we seek to accomplish the goals and plans envisioned for this year, this month, this week.

Excellent schools require a team of professionals who are relentlessly devoted to the mission and profoundly trust each other.

Teamwork begins by building trust. And the only way to do that is to overcome our need for invulnerability.
– Patrick Lencioni

Yes, we are responsible for guiding our schools in a constantly changing and more unforgiving environment.

Healthy schools with disciplined leadership always win in the long-term because they are more agile and responsive.

That's why we refuse to focus on factors that are outside of our control because there is no joy and serenity in that mindset.

Instead, we choose to ...

> ... **Courageously grow, owning our self-intelligence and growth.**
> ... **Constantly advance, building the quality and trust among our team.**
> ... **Consistently deliver, following up and following through on our promises.**

All fields of leadership require a level of discipline and resiliency. We accept that our commitment to equip, encourage, and engage our students demands even more collaboration and perseverance.

> *The way a team plays as a whole determines its success. You may have the greatest bunch of individual*
> *stars in the world, but if they don't play together, the club won't be worth a dime.*
> – Babe Ruth

We're willing to sacrifice comfort for the growth that is required of us individually and collectively.

Criticism and conflict come with the role, so we sustain a toughness to carry on while also remaining vulnerable enough to listen and empathetically understand.

Because that's what team players do.

Nurture and cultivate your team, inspiring an exponentially greater love for the work and for each other.

Love'em and Lead'em!

Active Question

Did I do my best to build and support our team today?

JOY NO MATTER WHAT

*I just wanted to have joy
no matter what happened tonight.*

—ALLYSON FELIX

It's easy to find inspiration at the Olympics, with so many people who devoted their lives to becoming the best in the world at their chosen sport.

The story of the American track phenom Allyson Felix is especially powerful because of...

*her discipline,
her durability, and
her demeanor.*

She is a champion because of who she is more than what she has accomplished athletically.

> *Each day holds a surprise. But only if we expect it
> can we see, hear, or feel it when it comes to us.
> Let's not be afraid to receive each day's surprise,
> whether it comes to us as sorrow or as joy.*
> --Henri Nouwen

Her workouts are famous, pushing her body to the max.

Allyson isn't comfortable just being in the race—she practices and prepares to win every one.

But, she also isn't afraid of losing—which has happened often. As a matter of fact, she said the losses provide the best lessons.

She has turned many disappointments into an extraordinarily long track career, even winning at the 2021 Summer Olympics after a very complicated, life-threatening pregnancy.

> *Focus on the journey,*
> *not the destination.*
> *Joy is found not in finishing*
> *an activity but in doing it.*
> — Greg Anderson

Win or lose, Allyson exudes a joy on her face and in her words.

That's a powerful testimony and model to inspire resilient education leadership.

What is the source of our joy?
Can we have joy no matter what?

We can overcome the pressure, the criticism, the surprises, and even those emotionally draining people by remembering who we are and staying connected to our purpose and source of joy.

May your joy be sustained as you seek to win, awakening gratitude and creativity in those around you.

Love'em and Lead'em!

Active Question

Did I do my best to lead with joy no matter what today?

OWN THE NARRATIVE

Storytelling is powerful. We can know a lot of things intellectually, but humans really live on storytelling. Primarily with ourselves; we're all stories of our own narrative.

— RICHARD LINKLATER

A useful exercise to discover our personal genius is to write out the table of contents of the autobiography of our lives.

What are the major chapters?
Who made the biggest impact during each phase?
What decisions were made and why?
In what areas was growth achieved, and what lessons were learned?

Knowing our story is how we own it and make conscious decisions about where we're going next. That's valuable self-intelligence!

We are all at the center of our own narrative, but it's a narrative that changes every time we retell it.
— Ruth Ware

The potential of our leadership is fully realized when we make our narrative authentic--as truthful as possible.

Crucial to our influence is the story that we tell and repeat.

Sometimes we deceive ourselves into yielding control to other people, a set of circumstances, an organizational system, or even a myth.

The dangerous repercussion of giving up that ownership is that we become "victims" and subject to those outside forces. If there's nothing that can be done, then we're free from our responsibilities to lead, teach, and overcome.

> *Watch out that no poisonous*
> *root of bitterness grows up to*
> *trouble you, corrupting many.*
> — Hebrews 12:15b

We each have our own path that winds in different directions.

But certain points of wisdom prevail regardless of our varying journeys.

Blaming other people or situations is a dead end street of bitterness and ignorance. Taking responsibility enables us to retain a critical attribute of intelligence: the ability to change.

The hallmark trait of highly effective educators is joyful adaptability.

Write your own story, boldly leading yourself first so that others can learn from the faithful testimony of your life.

Love'em and Lead'em!

BRING THE LIGHT

*People often say that motivation doesn't last.
Well, neither does bathing—that's why we
recommend it daily.*

—ZIG ZIGLAR

Our travel plans were disrupted by the weather. A leadership training workshop and a board retreat were postponed because the power was out for thousands of people across the region with frigid temperatures prevailing.

Life changes quickly when there's no electricity to produce heat and light. It's entertaining to rough it for a little while, but it can get old quickly.

We need light—it's a main source of energy, providing healthy nutrition as well as needed perspective. We're less productive and less pleasant without it.

*Darkness cannot drive out darkness; only light can do that.
Hate cannot drive out hate; only love can do that.*
—Martin Luther King, Jr.

As educators, our love for people and for learning lights the path for others to follow. Our clear vision and disciplined action illuminate the path forward.

We keep our faculty motivated because they change the world for our students.

We keep our students motivated because education is the pathway to a better future.

We keep our families motivated because we're walking this journey with them.

We keep our alumni motivated because their roots can produce new growth.

We keep our donors motivated because they can enable our vision.

> *No one after lighting a lamp covers*
> *it with a jar or puts it under a bed,*
> *but puts it on a stand, so that those*
> *who enter may see the light.*
> — Luke 8:16

As servant leaders, we pour into others even when they are less than appreciative.

They follow our leadership even when sometimes disagreeing with decisions because they trust us and can count on us to deliver on our promises.

We inspire them to commit to the mission, culture, and goals because this work is worth the sacrifices and the investment of energy.

By consistently sharing our light, we enable moments of great joy and fulfillment.

Shine brightly, my friend, daily motivating your colleagues, students, and others as you aspire to excellence.

Love'em and Lead'em!

Active Question

Did I take steps to motivate myself and my network of influence today?

CAN YOU SEE IT?

Never lose an opportunity of seeing anything
beautiful, for beauty is God's handwriting.

— RALPH WALDO EMERSON

Being home for the holidays allows more time for certain comfort foods.

For me, that includes creative ways to enjoy grits. I love them with cheese, onions, mushrooms, shrimp, gravy, and lots of other creative ingredients.

If you've only had the bland, porridge style of grits that most restaurants serve, then I can understand it if you don't care for them.

With the right type of stone-ground grits combined with expert preparation and great imagination, the possibilities are endlessly delicious.

I think you'd love my grits!

We all have possibilities we don't know about.
We can do things we don't even dream we can do.
— Dale Carnegie

Thinking in terms of possibilities rather than limitations is core to our calling.

What we see as educators depends on that for which we look.

Cynicism and sarcasm are often rooted in past hurt. While people with this mindset need our love, they should be working anywhere but in a school.

The value of wise educators isn't that they're so smart or have seen so much, but that they can inspire the imagination of others and energize their path.

> *Faith consists in believing when it is beyond the power of reason to believe.*
> — Voltaire

Learn to see with greater clarity, training your mind toward calmness and patience, deferring judgment in favor of love and wisdom.

See what others are missing.
See what everyone else chooses to avoid.
See them for the possibilities of the present, not the problems of the past.
See beyond fear, bias, and conformity.
See the world with fresh eyes each day, free from the burden of un-grace.
See the beauty and blessings all around you, and make some awesome memories.

(And maybe even enjoy some grits 😃)

Love'em and Lead'em!

Active Question

Did I do my best to see the people, not the problems today?

FINDING SERENITY

God grant me the serenity to accept
the things I cannot change,
the courage to change the things I can,
and the wisdom to know the difference.

— REINHOLD NIEBUHR

The Serenity Prayer above asks for calmness and peace in dealing with the challenges of life.

Some things can be changed, and come can't—Wisdom is found in knowing the difference.

You know by now that leadership is full of ups and downs-- and occasionally, you get hit by a big one.

A popular faculty member surprises you by announcing they've accepted another position.

One of your most loyal families decides to go in a different direction.

We call the last three months of the school year, *The Last Quarter Triangle.* (Can you hear the Twilight Zone music playing in the background?)

That's the time when energy tends to be at its lowest, relationships often unravel because some faculty and families will not be returning, and people start to "check out."

> *Curiosity endows the people who have it with a generosity in argument and a serenity in their own mode of life which springs from their cheerful willingness to let life take the form it will.*
> — Alistair Cooke

I saw a video posted on Instagram of a woman narrating her view of devastation around her house from heavy rains east of Nashville, TN. The water rose so high that most of her car and the first level of her house were flooded.

This area was hit hard over the previous few years with flooding and tornadoes. The trials just kept coming! Yet, there was no panic or fear in this woman's voice.

She clearly had a peace deep down inside and chose to own the situation rather than letting it own her.

From the challenges in her life (I did a little research and discovered she has also had to overcome an autoimmune disease), she developed a high degree of emotional intelligence with the ability to respond rather than react.

This woman was blessed with the serenity to accept the things she cannot change, the courage to change the things she can, and the wisdom to know the difference. And her testimony and influence were stronger as a result.

The advantage goes to those educators who are mindfully aware of their present reality but are also able to sustain serenity in their spirit because they choose to adapt to those factors that are outside their control.

May each day be full of great joy and peace for you, my friend, as you persevere through as a conqueror.

Love'em and Lead'em!

Active Question

Did I do my best to model wisdom and serenity today?

FALSE ASSUMPTIONS

Begin challenging your own assumptions.
Your assumptions are your windows on
the world. Scrub them off every once in while,
or the light won't come in.

— ALAN ALDA

More often than not, our assumptions get in the way of our success as educators.

Our made-up narratives usually limit genuine trust and understanding, sometimes triggering ungraceful reactions that undermine relationships.

One of our biggest mistakes is to believe our assumptions are true—regardless of the weakness in the evidence.

It's usually the things we think we know, without a factual basis, that lead us astray because we fail to ask the right questions out of an abundance of destructive overconfidence.

Separating the facts from assumptions increases the likelihood of us responding in wisdom and love.

(Check out the short animated story "The Present" for a powerful example.)

Assumptions are the
termites of relationships.
— Henry Winkler

In the Bible, Joshua 22 tells the story of a misunderstanding that almost escalated into a deadly battle. One group made erroneous assumptions about why the other group built a large structure, and they literally declared war!

Thankfully, the first group sent representatives to clarify the situation and learned that their assumptions were wrong. War was averted because they eventually asked clarifying questions.

In the pretense of righteousness, war is too often declared in and around schools—without even asking about real intent and seeking to understand.

We particularly saw this behavior during the Coronavirus pandemic.

No one sees the world objectively! Instead, we are all limited by the lens of our own fears, beliefs, and biases.

In order to sustain authentically excellent schools, we have to be more aware of our assumptions with humility and discernment. It's wise to be slow with anger and words.

I have learned throughout my life as a composer chiefly
through my mistakes and pursuits of false assumptions,
not by my exposure to founts of wisdom and knowledge.
— Igor Stravinsky

Because of our commitment to sustaining a healthy culture, we refuse to just complain about people who express different or opposing views.

Instead, we choose to listen and learn from them, avoiding destructive assumptions. This is a hard habit to learn but worth the investment.

Our influence with faculty and families is more authentic and impactful when we assume the best and seek to genuinely know them.

Communicate clearly and with an open mind, my friend, to create the best conditions for stronger relationships.

Love'em and Lead'em!

Active Question

Did I do my best to assume the best of others today?

STEP OUT IN FAITH

The human body has limitations.
The human spirit is boundless.

— DEAN KARNAZES

What's holding you back?

When you look at yourself in the mirror, what do you see?

Is it the real you?

Or does your internal narrative cloud the image?

We can do incredible things because our brains are ridiculously more complex than any computer invented so far.

As a matter of fact, engineers at Google and Harvard have endeavored to produce a searchable 3D map of the human brain in unprecedented detail.

They started with a very tiny sample of human cerebral cortex that represents about one-millionth of the entire brain.

Their analysis of that microscopic piece of tissue was startling!

"It contains 50,000 cells and 130 million synapses, as well as smaller segments of the cells such axons, dendrites, myelin and cilia. But perhaps the most stunning statistic is that the whole thing takes up 1.4 petabytes of data – that's more than a million gigabytes."

WOW!

As educators, we know that learning limitations too early can actually constrain inspiration and possibilities. So we must strive to maintain a balance in our messages and curriculum.

> *There are no limitations to the mind except those we acknowledge.*
> — Napoleon Hill

Self-intelligence remains a powerful ally, where we understand our natural talents, strengths, and even boundaries. Many limitations are fabricated, but some are real.

Your limitations can become strengths, enabling you to discover your personal genius and unique niche. Accurately understanding your limitations requires looking at the facts and being honest with yourself.

Is it time for you to move beyond the self-imposed limits that keep holding you back and take some bold steps?

Steps, not leaps. Instead of trying to make a major overhaul, start with small, manageable decisions. Incremental progress will lead to greater growth and joy!

Ask, and it will be given to you; seek, and you will find; knock, and it will be opened to you.

— Matthew 7:7

Sometimes you can truly only know who you are and what you're capable of when you see your options, step out in faith, and take a chance.

Love'em and Lead'em!

Active Question

Did I do my best to overcome self-imposed limitations today?

FACING OUR FEARS

What is defeat? Nothing but education.
Nothing but the first step to something better.

— WENDELL PHILLIPS

They say taking the first step is the most crucial.

It often requires overcoming fear and pain.

But that's how the recovery process begins.

Following knee surgery, a teacher friend had to go to physical therapy and came face-to-face with this reality.

She knew it was going to be hard, but when the therapist guided her over to the stairs to take that first step up, she felt overwhelmed.

He could sense her anxiety and what came next was true love.

Pulling down the mask that covered his face, he said with a smile,

"Mrs. Meyer, it's me, James. I was in your class for first grade, and I remember how you were always there for me, helping me learn with such kindness. You were there for me back then, and I'm here for you now."

After a few shared memories, a big hug, and some tears, she turned once again to conquer the pain of that first step with greater courage.

It was hard! It was painful! And it was necessary!

> *I have learned over the years that when one's mind is made up, this diminishes fear; knowing what must be done does away with fear.*
> — Rosa Parks

As Educators, we have to face our fears.

> Fear of resolving conflict with difficult people or situations.
> Fear of trying something new that's outside the comfort zone.
> Fear of becoming someone new, different than before.

With the love and support of others on this journey with us, we choose to move forward and do what must be done.

> *Love is patient, Love is kind.*
> —I Corinthians 13:4a

This path isn't easy—that's why so many choose a different way.

But, we are committed to love and lead people through education because of the life-changing possibilities. Fulfilling that calling requires us to daily be patient, kind, and particularly full of grace.

Faithfully, and even stubbornly, we press onward in this journey of growth and transformation because we never know when we'll encounter those we teach.

Turn your fears into opportunities to grow, my friend, courageously doing what must be done.

Love'em and Lead'em!

Active Question

Did I do my best to face my fears today?

ENCOURAGEMENT FROM A FUNERAL

The fear of death follows
from the fear of life.
A man who lives fully is
prepared to die at any time.

— MARK TWAIN

I had the honor of leading the funeral for a family member.

The message focused on love and hope as those gathered had the opportunity to celebrate many wonderful memories and reflect on what matters most in life.

We tried not to make this a rushed event that was merely an inconvenience, preferring instead to acknowledge the reality of our loss and the grief experienced.

Attending a funeral teaches multiple and value lessons for life. It's healthy for our heart, mind, and soul as we regain perspective and come face-to-face with our own mortality.

Life is Short and Precious!

> *You have to learn to see things*
> *in the right proportions.*
> *Learn to see great things great*
> *and small things small.*
> — Corrie Ten Boom

In these moments, we're forced to be starkly aware of our own approaching deadline. Our limitations can get lost in the hectic pace of our work as educators, but there's no death-denying at a funeral.

A tombstone is typically engraved with a date of birth and a date of death. In between those dates is a very important dash. That deceptively simple mark cannot begin to communicate all that happened in those intervening years.

What's in your dash?

We need those powerful reminders of earnestly facing death to focus because what we see in life depends significantly on that for which we look.

> *Life is 10 percent what you make it*
> *and 90 percent how you take it.*
> — Irving Berlin

Remember that the best things in life and leadership actually aren't things at all but rather the human connections, inspirations, and joyful memories made.

Unresolved conflict is a poison to relationships, so make the extra effort to humbly reconnect and heal.

Unspoken words of appreciation and encouragement have no value, so become intentional about frequently expressing love.

Ungrace is a lonely path of pain, with forgiveness withheld and joyful reunion lost.

Time is too precious to be lost in self-inflicted disconnection.

Greet every morning with a sense of gratitude and purpose, and make the most of every opportunity to renew and restore.

Love'em and Lead'em!

Active Question

Did I do my best to live with purpose and perspective today?

THE "ELEVATER" SPEECH

*Our chief want is someone who will inspire us
to be what we know we could be.*

— RALPH WALDO EMERSON

The last quarter of the school year is perhaps the most difficult season of all.

This is a period in which our relational ecosystem loses energy and becomes more fragile.

Spring fever starts to kick in, with even the students becoming more distracted.

Some people will be moving on because of graduation or a relocation.

Some others won't be returning for other reasons, so they begin to disconnect.

The pace of the schedule accelerates with teachers having to finish the curriculum, end-of-year traditions, and intense preparations for next year well underway.

That's why we must intentionally step up to this leadership challenge to sustain energy and engagement!

The road to excellence cannot be walked alone, so we choose to work in unity with like-minded people and invest in them to authentically deliver on our mission.

Educators are motivators!

Motivation comes from working together with people we care about to achieve meaningful outcomes. We use words that inspire others, overtly expressing appreciation for teachers, staff, students, parents, volunteers, administrators, board members, donors, etc.

Nothing is as motivating as a few wisely-chosen, well-timed words of praise.

Our words of encouragement can inspire others to sustain their calling all the way to the last day of school.

Let everything you say be good and helpful, so that your words will be an encouragement to those who hear them.
– Ephesians 4:29

We will prevail because of our joyful attitude and determined focus.

It's recommended to have a compelling "Elevator Speech" about our school to invite others to join us, but we also need to have that "Elevater" Speech that encourages, lifts people up, and consistently communicates our genuine love and appreciation for them.

The words we use can be life-changing! They are one of the most powerful tools available to educators, so we wisely choose to use this power constructively to build up our students, colleagues, and parents.

We seek to inspire people because, in the end, we want them to look at us and say, "Because of you, I didn't give up."

Elevate your leadership, demonstrating every day how much you believe in them.

Love'em and Lead'em!

Active Question

Did I do my best to encourage and inspire the people around me today?

TRUE LOVE DOES

Love does not begin and end the
way we seem to think it does.
Love is a battle, love is a war;
love is a growing up.

— JAMES BALDWIN

Valentine's Day is our designated time to celebrate love by giving cards, gifts, flowers, candy, etc.

People actually make some big investments to show love—especially in the U.S.

About 145,000,000 cards will be exchanged by people of all ages on February 14.

(Fun fact: The first known valentine was sent in 1415 by a Duke named Charles to his wife.)

Over 250,000,000 flowers are prepared around the world just for this special day.

At present, almost $30,000,000,000 will be spent by Americans alone to celebrate love on this day. Wow—Love is a big business!

Love doesn't make the world go 'round.
Love is what makes the ride worthwhile.
— Franklin P. Jones

Truly, Love is our business!

True Love moves beyond curriculum, lesson plans, and chaotic schedules to knowing and providing what they need—starting with the educators on our team.

True love makes the work and sacrifices of this life worth doing.

Love, true love, will follow you forever (for those Princess Bride fans...).

The love of educators can transform hearts and minds, showing that true love is not only for the future but lives in the present. It's our most powerful skill!

Be completely humble and gentle;
be patient, bearing with one another in love.
—Ephesians 4:2

As we grow as servant-leaders, so grows our influence and our testimony.

We take responsibility for our life and mission, creating beauty even in the midst of messy conflict and ugly behavior.

We're busy but never too busy to prioritize relationships and stay connected with those who matter most and need us most.

Because often it's the small moments of genuine care that have the greatest impact.

Make each day unforgettable for those whom you're called to serve, remembering how very much you are loved.

Love'em and Lead'em!

Active Question

Did I grow in my capacity to truly love others today?

LEADERS ARE READERS

If we encounter a man of rare intellect,
we should ask him what books he reads.

— RALPH WALDO EMERSON

We love visiting schools to learn from their history, data, and people. Each one has a unique story and organizational context: mission, target market, core values, etc.

It's especially interesting to see what books are on the shelves of the leaders.

We love seeing books that represent a broad perspective because it's indicative of someone who has a growth mindset and seeks to learn innovative best practices.

Reading is a critical discipline for educators, but a chaotically busy schedule chokes off vital sources of inspiration and insight that we desperately need.

> *You don't have to burn books to destroy a culture.*
> *Just get people to stop reading them.*
> — Ray Bradbury

What are the last three books you've read to elevate your capacity to love and to lead?

That's one of my favorite interview questions to ask because the answer reveals a person's level of curiosity and commitment to grow.

Some people can't remember the last books they read. Others respond with great enthusiasm about what they've read and learned. We want the latter.

An educator without well-worn books lacks zeal for the work.

> *Do not conform to the pattern of this world, but be transformed by the renewing of your mind.*
> — Romans 12:2

It's our deep love for people and for learning that fuels us.

Every leader is tempted to give up, settling for compromise and mediocrity.

In those moments of fear, self-doubt, or frustration, we choose to convert that negative energy into fuel that drives us forward to excellence.

Instead of wasting time worrying about the "what ifs," we continuously study and learn to enhance the experience of our faculty, students and families.

Never stop reading! Read a page a day or a chapter a day. Just read.

Renew your mind as a disciplined reader, my friend, enhancing your imagination and wisdom.

Love'em and Lead'em!

Active Question

Did I make time to read good stuff today?

DREAM SPECIFICALLY

We become what we think about
most of the time, and that's
the strangest secret.

— EARL NIGHTINGALE

Dreams are an integral part of how our brains function.

Everybody dreams while sleeping, but we forget most of them.

Falling is one of the most common dreams.

Being chased is another.

We were made to dream!

Not just while sleeping, but most certainly as part of our calling as educators.

Perhaps our greatest contribution is pursuing a powerful vision for our institutions that goes beyond the status quo to inspire true excellence in teaching and learning.

I would rather die of passion
than of boredom.
— Vincent van Gogh

People with dreams and goals have more energy and are happier.

Without a dream, it's hard to be enthusiastic or inspired about this work.

People who lack passion and enthusiasm aren't effective educators because they're working for the paycheck and just stumbling through life.

We have to be extremely careful in our influence to never discourage our students or our faculty from dreaming and pursuing their dreams.

Dream-killers should be working anywhere but in schools.

> *Every great dream begins with a dreamer. Always remember, you have within you the strength, the patience, and the passion to reach for the stars to change the world.*
> — Harriet Tubman

The dreams we're talking about aren't just vague fantasies—they are specific imagined futures that make life better than it is today.

Where are we leading our people? Is it worth it for them to follow our lead?

Can they trust our vision and that we have the discipline to follow through?

Our dreams will only be realized when our habits are fully aligned with our goals—both our individual habits and our organizational habits.

Dream big and specifically, my friend, combining your vision with the habits that will make them real.

Love'em and Lead'em!

Active Question

Did I practice the habits necessary to achieve my dreams today?

BEYOND THE FAMILIAR

If you go back a few hundred years, what we take for granted today would seem like magic - being able to talk to people over long distances, to transmit images, flying, accessing vast amounts of data like an oracle. These are all things that would have been considered magic a few hundred years ago.

— ELON MUSK

Nothing damages our vision more than familiarity. It's an affliction that ruins our ability to see the beauty and the incredible people all around us.

We take time for granted.

We take people for granted.

We take abilities for granted.

We take freedom for granted.

It's a weird paradox: The more visible they are, the more invisible they become.

We can become blind by seeing each day as a similar one.

Each day is a different one, each
day brings a miracle of its own.
It's just a matter of paying
attention to this miracle.
— Paulo Coelho

How quickly we can forget the amazing times in our lives when we truly experienced miracles— when we were delivered from painful people and circumstances.

We need those moments that spark our minds and reset our perspective.

That's when we remember to see--hopefully before it's too late.

Remember the joy of making someone smile, of listening to a friend, of being alive!

Be present in those moments and grasp the beauty that's all around you.

Happiness cannot be traveled to, owned, earned, worn or consumed. Happiness is the spiritual experience of living every minute with love, grace, and gratitude.
— Denis Waitley

Core to our calling is building a community in which people can thrive.

Even the most intense feelings of loyalty and commitment will fade when neglected and taken for granted. We have to guard against familiarity and complacency.

We don't do this work of education merely to make a living.

We cause people in our sphere of influence to love learning and each other.

We enable them to see greater possibilities and pursue an aspirational future.

Thank you for your commitment, my friend, to change lives as an educator.

Love'em and Lead'em!

Active Question

Did I do my best to appreciate the beauty of people and life today?

THE TIMING OF LIFE AND LEADERSHIP

*You don't have to swing hard
to hit a home run. If you got the timing, it'll go.*

— YOGI BERRA

Have you noticed that timing is the key to many things in life?

The key to great cooking is timing.
The key to great comedy is timing.
The key to great hitting is timing.
The key to great music is timing.
The key to great communication is timing.
The key to great relationships is timing.
The key to great leadership is timing.

> *For everything there is a season,
> and a time for every matter
> under heaven.*
> — Ecclesiastes 3:1

Sometimes it just feels like our timing is off. We're just not in the flow.

Maybe we need more practice, or perhaps things around us have changed that require adjustments to get back into rhythm.

Or, we may have to learn to trust.

We want our schedule to work as planned, but wisdom recognizes divine timing.

Our faith is strengthened when we find the courage to not always be in control, knowing that a greater plan will prevail and that we can flow with it to discover a deeper joy in contentment.

> *Comedy is not funny.*
> *Comedy is hard work*
> *and timing and lots*
> *and lots of rehearsals.*
> — Larry Hagman

Being able to choose the right moment for a decision and communicating it effectively is often determined by discipline and preparation.

We have to sustain a sharp mind and a high degree of emotional intelligence combined with social awareness to choose our timing wisely.

Getting the timing right can be hard work that requires practice and sometimes a good mentor to provide feedback—but those moments of inspired execution are worth it.

Be prepared to make greatness happen, my friend, recognizing the opportunities to adjust your timing as you encounter the people you're called to serve.

Love'em and Lead'em!

Active Question

Did I do my best to adjust my timing and get in the flow today?

SMILE POWER

What sunshine is to flowers, smiles are to humanity. These are but trifles, to be sure; but scattered along life's pathway, the good they do is inconceivable.

—JOSEPH ADDISON

Few things in the world are more powerful than a smile.

This simple expression of optimism and hope changes people because it creates a positive countenance that makes others feel safe and comfortable.

Regardless of what's happening around us, we can find a reason to smile.

According to the research of Harvard psychology professor Daniel Gilbert, we are very resilient with a remarkable ability to make the best of things. We've all witnessed people who have suffered a setback, tragedy, or disease, and yet they found a way to overcome and reclaim their joy.

A cheerful look brings joy to the heart; good news makes for good health.
—Proverbs 15:30

We have to be ready—in season and out of season—to encourage and inspire.

As educators, we're always bumping up against people or situations that create stress, but we are at our best when we search for those things that make life better. Our influence is too important to lose that perspective.

Students can learn that attitude from the example of their teachers.

Our smile is crucial to our love for people and creating the best environment.

> *Wear a smile and have friends; wear a scowl and have wrinkles.*
> —George Eliot

It's just better to lead and teach with a smile.

Happy people have a huge advantage.
Happy people are healthier and live longer.
Happy people have more friends and stronger relationships.
Happy people are more creative and more productive.

So Smile, because your influence is changing lives every day.

Love'em and Lead'em!

Active Question

Did I do my best to smile today?

THE LIFE CHANGING WISDOM
OF AN EDUCATOR

*The fool doth think he is wise, but
the wise man knows himself to be a fool.*

— WILLIAM SHAKESPEARE IN "AS YOU LIKE IT"

Dr. Ben Nesbit is a retired education leader for whom I will be eternally thankful.

He received many awards and accolades throughout his tenure as an educational leader in Columbia, SC. It was his wisdom that made him so appreciated among educators and students.

It takes intelligence to be an educator and even more to be a leader of educators. We work hard, are able to learn and solve problems, and make difficult decisions.

The best have also developed a wisdom found only in the scars of humility.

Dr. Nesbit genuinely listened to his faculty, students, and parents greater trusts.

He built relationships, provided encouragement, and was present at the right times. His wisdom and influence made an impact on my life, and now I seek to do the same.

> *God will not look you*
> *over for medals, degrees*
> *or diplomas but for scars.*
> — Elbert Hubbard

Wisdom is extremely valuable—literally a life-changer!

It's beyond being merely smart, clever, or shrewd.

Wisdom is...

- ... Understanding
- ... Prudence
- ... Discernment
- ... Foresight
- ... Self-control
- ... Adaptability
- ... Persistence.

We gain wisdom through reading, reflection, observation, prayer, and experience.

Wisdom enables us to let go of the ideal in order to embrace the reality of what is and then respond in an honorable and noble manner.

> *Yesterday I was clever, so*
> *I wanted to change the world.*
> *Today I am wise, so*
> *I am changing myself.*
> — Rumi

Life is lived with actions, not in words.
What we think is nice, but it's what we do that really matters.

Renew your pursuit of wisdom, my friend, because the decisions, words, and actions of an educator have eternal influence. Thank you for your enduring courage and commitment.

Love'em and Lead'em!

Active Question

Did I do my best to model and pursue wisdom today?

EDUCATORS LIVE LONGER

You might not always get what you want,
but you always get what you expect.

— CHARLES SPURGEON

Did you know that educators have an unusually long lifespan?

According to the Society of Actuaries, male educators live to about eighty-eight years old, while females live on average 90 years.

That's the opposite of what I would expect because of the stresses of this work.

Perhaps we live longer because we change lives, always keeping our expectations high.

Maybe we live longer because we continuously persevere, intelligently finding new solutions and pathways to achieve the goals.

Or we could live longer because we expect the best from people, believing in their potential and ability to grow.

The tongue has the power of life and death, and those who love it will eat its fruit.

As educators, our words can either energize life or they can kill the spirit.

Our tongues can build others up or can tear them down.

Sarcasm, gossip, and prejudice can infect our influence and culture, undermining the healthy ecosystem needed to grow.

We understand the power and temptations of our words, making it vital that we constantly are on our guard so that we speak wisdom and truth.

Acts of kindness and words of gratitude ease anxiety and reduce stress, leading to longer life and greater joy!

Educators are more than just dispensers of curriculum—we are enablers of great dreams!

Excellent leadership is never an accident—it's the result of intelligent discipline with great expectations.

A life is not important except in the impact it has on other lives.
— Jackie Robinson

Faith gives us inner strength and a healthy perspective in life.

Emotional intelligence is core to our ability to sustain relationships. That's what enables us to turn even difficult times into opportunities for growth.

We focus on the facts of the situation and how we are interpreting those facts, checking our own lens with a high degree of self-awareness.

We know how to flip the lens to see things from another point of view, understanding their feelings and needs.

We pursue and inspire great expectations because our influence is life changing!

Be the leader you were called to be, my friend, expecting the best of yourself and those who follow you.

Love'em and Lead'em!

Active Question

Did I do my best to pursue great expectations today?

LISTEN TO ADVICE

*It takes a great person
to give sound advice tactfully,
but a greater to accept it graciously.*

— LOGAN P. SMITH

A big part of our contribution as educators is providing feedback and advice.

You are not in this position because you're perfect nor the smartest in the school. (though at least one of those may be true 😜)

But you have demonstrated a level of wisdom and influence that others believed in you enough to follow your lead.

Well done!

How you mentor and develop the people around you is critical to your success and the mission of the school. And that begins with how you are mentored.

> *You know how advice is. You only want it if it agrees with what you wanted to do anyway.*
> — John Steinbeck

Some people receive advice graciously, and many don't.

How do you demonstrate humility and a desire to learn? By seeking advice and using it to improve.

- **Start listening**—Genuinely and thoughtfully listening. Start the day by listening. End the day by listening.

- **Share Your Goals**—Let your leadership and colleagues know what your growth plan goals are, along with why and how you are pursuing them.

- **Engage with a coach/mentor** who will give you sage advice and sometimes be quite direct in pushing you forward.

- **Don't make excuses**, especially by blaming others or predecessors--that's a fast way to kill culture.

Improve your habits and behaviors based on the advice you receive because nothing is more powerful for your peers, students, and families than a living example of a leader who is learning and growing.

Attitude is the key factor in the maturity of an educator, improving both personal and professional success.

> *The way of a fool is right in his own eyes, but a wise man is he who listens to counsel.*
> — Proverbs 12:15

The best educators are not only open to advice, but they ask for it out of a desire to grow. This is one of, *The Key Intelligences of Highly Effective Educators.*

That requires us to be present and available, intentionally planning our time accordingly.

Advice is most effectively received when it is expressed respectfully, includes a relevant story or analogy, and provides a specific call to action.

Be the model for others to follow, growing through wisdom and advice as an authentic leader.

Love'em and Lead'em!

Active Question

Did I do my best to seek and genuinely receive advice today?

AGILITY AND THE EDUCATOR

The pessimist complains about the wind;
the optimist expects it to change;
the realist adjusts the sails.

— WILLIAM ARTHUR WARD

I recently switched to a new dentist. The previous dentist had an unfriendly person at the reception desk, and I didn't care for the quality of services. (Don't underestimate the importance of kindness at the front.)

When I arrived for my appointment at the new dentist, they required several pages of paperwork. Most of it was the typical medical stuff, but when I reached the end of the fourth page, it included two page-long columns of "Yes/No" questions.

I was amused to read a few of them:

ARE YOU:

 ... considered a touchy person.
 ... often unhappy or depressed.
 ... frequently angry or upset.

After completing the paperwork, I walked back up to the counter and asked with a smile whether my answers to those questions would influence my continuation as a new patient.

The office manager laughed and said that never really came up, but the answers did help them make adjustments to their service approach.

Very interesting!

> *I cannot say whether things*
> *will get better if we change;*
> *what I can say is they must*
> *change if they are to get better.*
> – Georg C. Lichtenburg

The ability to adapt and negotiate is core to the educator's toolbox.

Every successful leader has to make the transition from a world of predictable behavior to one primarily defined by rapid and constant unpredictability.

We have to adjust to what our people need and to the situation in the moment while still maintaining our principles, integrity, and sanity.

Sometimes we need help from others to help us figure out how to adapt more effectively to various situations. And that's okay. **Ask!**

We can't make this happen alone–we need relationships with friends and advisors to help us sometimes navigate very difficult conditions.

Just like we encourage our students to seek help for both challenges in learning and in life, it makes sense for us to model that wisdom.

> *Plans fail for lack of counsel, but*
> *with many advisers they succeed*
> – Proverbs 15:22

The greatest danger we face isn't difficult people or a crisis situation—it's our inability to listen, learn, and adapt.

Keep growing, my friend, because that's where joy is found in this work.

Love'em and Lead'em!

Active Question

Did I do my best today to learn and adapt today?

DECISIVE LEADERSHIP

I'd rather regret the things I've done
than regret the things I haven't done.

— LUCILLE BALL

We frequently travel in our efforts to encourage and elevate those who educate—especially at the beginning of a new year. Our goal is to help them start with greater unity and exciting momentum.

On one trip to Texas, we met a woman who ran a jewelry store. Her creations were truly beautiful, and you could tell she really enjoyed her work.

We looked through the displays of necklaces, earrings, and other items, and I asked her what she did before opening her store.

She replied, "I was a teacher for many years and then became an administrator."

As you might expect, my eyes lit up, and I smiled big.

"Really! Wow, thank you for your service in education! Do you miss school life?"

She looked at me directly in the eyes, paused thoughtfully, and said:

"No, I really don't. It's an emotionally exhausting job that is under-appreciated."

> *Of all the words of*
> *mice and men,*
> *the saddest are,*
> *"It might have been."*
> — Kurt Vonnegut

This teacher turned entrepreneur went on to explain that conflict and dysfunction had infected the school leadership and culture for too many years.

In those last days of her tenure, some of the administrators expressed deep regrets about not making needed changes and allowing people to undermine the mission and goals.

We purchased a necklace for Tammy that was just right, along with some earrings. They're made of a unique shell with a deep reflective blue shine. Very nice! She has definitely found a great way to use her artistic abilities.

> *Decisiveness is a characteristic of high-performing men and*
> *women. Almost any decision is better than no decision at all.*
> — Brian Tracy

As we left the store, I wondered if it could have been different for her and her school.

Could her passion as an educator have been sustained, even through the stresses of the job, with disciplined, action-oriented leadership?

What if she had been encouraged and given constructive feedback?

What if the leadership had the commitment to create a culture of trust?

What if they had taken the steps to become truly authentic?

Or perhaps this business was where she needed to be all along.

Take advantage of opportunities to lead forward, my friend, with a commitment toward action and no regrets.

Love'em and Lead'em!

Active Question

Did I do my best to lead decisively today?

KINDNESS CHANGES PEOPLE

Kindness boggles my mind.
It's the only force in nature that increases
simultaneously for the giver and the receiver.

– DANIEL LUBETZKY

Over the last couple of weeks, I've encountered some people whose kindness and commitment to high-quality service made me smile.

One was a restaurant server who was distinctive in her smile and joyful personality.

Another was a business owner who obviously enjoyed his work and taking care of his customers.

I literally felt happier as a result of their kindness.

Beginning today, treat everyone you meet as if they were going to be dead by midnight. Extend to them all the care, kindness and understanding you can muster, and do it with no thought of any reward. Your life will never be the same again.

– Og Mandino

As educators, we have to carefully avoid falling into the unproductive trap of trying to judge who is worthy of our kindness and who isn't.

Unconditional love is fundamental to our calling.

Kindness is core to our commitment to teach and inspire.

We show it through acceptance, a genuine smile, supportive gestures, thoughtfulness—the possibilities are endless and entirely up to us.

We choose to treat each employee, student, and parent with kindness and joy.

> *First and foremost, we need to be*
> *the adults we want our children to be.*
> *We should watch our own gossiping*
> *and anger. We should model the*
> *kindness we want to see.*
> – Brene Brown

Some advocate for random kindness.
Even more important in our schools is...

... Consistent Kindness
> Where our entire organization delivers a life-changing
> experience.

... Ridiculous Kindness
> Going the extra mile for even those who constantly
> criticize or seek to undermine our work.

... Generous Kindness

Giving boldly with no expectation of reciprocation.

Let your light shine brightly, my friend, modeling kindness as you build a culture of authentic excellence.

Love'em and Lead'em!

Active Question

Did I do my best to be boldly kind today?

LEADING WITH HARMONY

Happiness is not a matter
of intensity but of balance,
order, rhythm, and harmony.

– THOMAS MERTON

Harmony isn't the first word that comes to mind when we think of education leadership.

It most likely isn't the second, third, or even fourth.

As a matter of fact, harmony seldom makes the top 20!

Especially these days.

Yet, great joy is found in harmony.

Harmony within ourselves and with our faith, family, friends, and faculty.

> *If we have no peace, it is because we have*
> *forgotten that we belong to each other.*
> – Mother Teresa

People living and working in harmony with each other are peaceful rather than mired in selfish battles. That doesn't happen without determined educators like you.

If we're unable to foster harmony among our colleagues with deep trust across the organization, our leadership style is obsolete.

Our people need the beauty of unity and peace that only happens through disciplined leadership that is resilient.

> *Live in harmony with one another. Do not be proud,*
> *but be willing to associate with people of low position.*
> *Do not be conceited.*
> – Romans 12:16

We choose to lead with vision and passion, refusing to be afraid of any challenge.

We choose to lead forward with courage and integrity, refusing to allow conflict and dysfunctional behaviors to infect our culture and degrade our mission.

We choose to lead with humility and grace, rejecting the destructive mindset that disrupts harmony.

May you be blessed with rhythm and harmony as you model a joy for teaching and learning.

Love'em and Lead'em!

Active Question

Did I do my best to live and lead in harmony today?

KNOW YOUR REAL ANTAGONIST

He that wrestles with us strengthens
our nerves and sharpens our skill.
Our antagonist is our helper.

– EDMUND BURKE

Where would we be without our villains?

We may not love them, but villains are critical parts of the stories we enjoy.

Voldemort made Harry Potter the hero he became.

Lady Macbeth was the one with the brains and ambition.

Those Dalmatians were just spotty K-9s without Cruella Deville.

Expert storytellers know that the antagonist is the character who most stands in the way of the protagonist achieving the desired goals by creating conflicts and problems.

It's that tension that makes the story interesting.

A well-developed antagonist puts up a spectacular fight but is defeated in the end.

> *Nobody is a villain in their own story.*
> *We're all the heroes of our own stories.*
> — George R. R. Martin

We all have stories that we use to express our state of affairs.

Who is the antagonist in our education journey?

Board members?
Administrators?
Faculty members?
Students?
Parents?

Hope not—because healthy schools are frankly impossible when we're living in conflict among ourselves, unable to love and trust each other.

Too often, we are our own worst enemy, turning on each other rather than sustaining the deep relationships required to lead strong. This produces dysfunctional behaviors and systems that steal the joy of teaching and learning.

Educators who accomplish authentic excellence coalesce into a unified team and focus on the real barriers and issues. Their stories reflect a cohesive courage that learns from those who pose resistance, growing individually and collectively.

Create a powerful narrative that inspires excellence!

Pick your antagonist wisely, my friend, refusing to allow destructive attitudes to limit your success.

Love'em and Lead'em!

Active Question

Did I do my best to create the best story today?

CONTAGIOUS COURAGE

Courage is more exhilarating than fear
and in the long run it is easier.

— ELEANOR ROOSEVELT

We're not just making a living as educators—we're changing lives!

We make the world a better place through our influence and performance.

By choosing courage over fear, we enable people to achieve

> greater vision,
>> greater hope, and
>>> greater success.

Our passion is contagious!

We refuse to be sucked into a rut of mediocrity, opting instead to pursue a burning passion for cultivating an incredible team of educators and then loving them like they are.

You will never do anything in this world without courage. It is the greatest quality of the mind next to honor.
— Aristotle

Courageous leaders know how to stay focused on what's most important to genuinely grow, ensuring shared vision and clear accountability.

Sure, some may think we're a little crazy to keep raising the bar and expecting more, but that relentless passion helps us stay motivated because growth only happens when leaders push through the barriers to change things for the better.

Courage is not the absence of fear, but the mastery of it.
— Mark Twain

Whenever we encounter an authentically excellent school, we know that a courageous leadership team once became united.

People don't become what they ought to be by remaining where they are and what they are—they change because they're supposed to change.

We engage and unite people because that's how we fulfill our calling and mission.

We take people on a journey where they don't necessarily want to go--at least not at first--but it's necessary to make our collective narrative authentic.

Let them think you're a little fanatical, my friend, as you courageously deliver on your promises and build a team capable of excellence.

Love'em and Lead'em!

Active Question

Did I do my best to courageously cultivate a united team today?

DREAM-KILLER HABITS

All our dreams can come true,
if we have the courage to pursue them.

– WALT DISNEY

What limits our success as educators?

Doubt.

Guilt.

A sense of unworthiness.

Procrastination.

Incessant distraction.
(one of my most insidious limiters ...)
These habits are dream-killers!

Lots of people are passionate about education, but so many undermine themselves, remaining hopelessly stuck and wishing what could be.

Being conscious of our self-imposed limitations is critical to our growth.

We have the ability to consciously change our future by making different choices.

As we exercise the discipline to renew our minds, we take ownership of our destiny.

> *We are put on this planet only once,*
> *and to limit ourselves to the familiar*
> *is a crime against our minds.*
> — Roger Ebert

When we change self-limiting behaviors, we're able to aspire to a greater purpose.

So, how do we avoid those negative mindsets and habits that limit our success?

Take ownership and responsibility.

> No excuses—no blame. That's how we most use our talents to love others.

Take the first step with bold action.

> Progress elevates confidence, so stop waiting on the perfect time or situation and start taking those first action steps.

Figure out how to get the help needed without asking for handouts.

> Connect with people who have taken that path and find the resources needed to overcome the obstacles.

Failure isn't the opposite of success—it's part of the journey of achieving our goals.

Limiting beliefs lead to limiting thoughts.
Limiting thoughts lead to limiting actions.
Change your beliefs and watch your actions change.
— Dr. Charles F. Glassman

Mediocrity is a popular place because it's safe.

Chronic self-doubt is a plague that may have started early in life, but (good news) it can still be eradicated. Doubt kills more dreams than anything else.

Please don't give up on creating new pathways to love students, parents, and fellow educators.

Our job is to inspire them, to bring our 'A-game every day, and urge them forward. We have to keep pushing open those heavy doors to life for the next generation.

Learn from everything and everyone, and let your courage catch up with your calling.

Love'em and Lead'em!

Active Question

Did I do my best to renew my mind today?

LESSONS FROM A VETERAN EDUCATOR

My own definition of leadership is this:
The capacity and the will to rally men
and women to a common purpose and the character which
inspires confidence.

— GENERAL B.L. MONTGOMERY

While at a family event, I met an experienced veteran. Tom served as an educator for over thirty years and recently retired.

I thanked him for his service, to which he smiled gratefully. And then, I asked him about his work as an educator.

What I really wanted to know was whether he was a manager or a leader and what insights he learned that most contributed to his success.

You manage things; you lead people.
— Rear Admiral Grace Murray Hopper

I could tell by his spirit and demeanor that he loved his job as a leader of educators. He wasn't jaded nor fed up with the system.

The hardest part, he said, was building the best team of educators, recognizing that there is a difference between having the credentials to teach and having the gift and talents to be effective in the role.

He was willing to do whatever was necessary to expel toxic under-performers.

That required developing a thick skin without being hard-hearted—a tough balance to maintain in this emotionally draining work.

Despite the many barriers to making these hard decisions, he persevered.

> *Men make history and not the other way around. In periods where there is no leadership, society stands still. Progress occurs when courageous, skillful leaders seize the opportunity to change things for the better.*
> —Harry S. Truman

My new friend also emphasized that a healthy culture is the key to an excellent school, providing the best environment for educators and students to thrive.

A group of talented, energized, engaged educators can change the world, but only if they reach a level of almost mystical devotion to the mission and to each other.

That only happens when education leaders do more than point the way--they exercise the disciplines that create a progressive journey of authentic excellence.

I was standing in the presence of a truly courageous educator!

Be the leader you were created to be, my friend, rallying those who follow you through a compelling vision with the character that inspires confidence.

Love'em and Lead'em!

Active Question

Did I do my best today to build the leadership capacity of others?

THE PRIVILEGE OF PRESSURE

*Pressure is a privilege —it only
comes to those who earn it.*

— BILLIE JEAN KING

I love watching swimming during the Olympics, and in the 2021 Summer Games, a rare event occurred: Three Olympic record-setting swims took place consecutively during the women's 100m backstroke qualifying heats.

First, Canada's Kylie Masse set a new mark, then American Regan Smith beat her record in the next heat, and then reigning World Record holder Kaylee McKeown of Australia beat that with a new record.

Wow!

*God changes caterpillars into butterflies,
sand into pearls and coal into diamonds
using time and pressure. He's working on you, too.*
— Rick Warren

One interesting story that was shared during the TV broadcast was about Regan Smith. They showed a picture of her school yearbook from 4th grade, where she made a bold prediction.

Beneath her name was the title: Olympian.

She boldly and publicly set a goal and then put pressure on herself to achieve it.

We are Educators!

In this profession, pressure is inescapable. We all know people who complain under tough circumstances and find ways to escape leadership rather than transform that pressure into motivating energy.

Like those Olympic athletes, we eat pressure for breakfast because we know that it refines us and makes us stronger.

> *An artist never works under ideal conditions. If they existed, his work wouldn't exist, for the artist doesn't live in a vacuum. Some sort of pressure must exist. The artist exists because the world is not perfect. Art would be useless if the world were perfect, as man wouldn't look for harmony but would simply live in it.*
> — Andrei Tarkovsky

Be the creative leader that you are. Remember that pressure is a privilege. Refuse to get sucked into that hectic lifestyle where the tyranny of the urgent prevails.

Yes, we're always busy and under pressure from a multitude of factors.

But, make and take the time to breathe.

Remember your purpose as an educator.

Restore your perspective to refocus on what matters most.

Regain your footing as you fulfill your noble calling.

Keep your sights on the goal, choosing to lead with more love and more passion than your community has ever imagined.

Love'em and Lead'em!

Active Question

Did I do my best to turn pressure into positive energy today?

THE MAGIC OF PATIENCE

Patience and perseverance have a
magical effect before which difficulties
disappear and obstacles vanish.

— JOHN QUINCY ADAMS

"Nothing comes easy in this world."

That's what John Rahm said after winning the 2021 U.S. Open Golf Championship.

He has faced much adversity in his life, especially over the preceding few months, but his attitude stayed focused on the possibilities ahead rather than the pain of the past.

His patience and positive attitude helped make him a champion.

Patience is truly a virtue.

It's the ability to cope with annoyance, disappointment, and/or pain without losing our purpose or self-control. Part of the magical effect of patience is that it gives us the ability to find a path through the challenges with greater creativity, collaboration, and productivity.

145

Patience isn't just the ability to "wait it out"--it's also the attitude we display.

No patience, no grit.

No patience, no wisdom.

No patience, no serenity.

> *We could never learn to be brave and patient, if there were only joy in the world.*
> — Helen Keller

No matter who you are or what you know, you are going to suffer through setbacks and conflict--especially in this work of education. Happiness has no meaning if not balanced against these difficult times in life.

Excellence is achieved not by strength but by patient perseverance.

> *A moment of patience can prevent a great disaster and a moment of impatience can ruin a whole life.*
> — Chinese Proverb

It's sometimes hard to understand why some things happen the way they do, but that's where we get to patiently allow events to unfold and courageously press on.

Emotionally reacting to that board issue, parent turmoil, or difficult employee contributes to dysfunction and undermines our executive presence.

Instead, let's choose to persevere through the exercise of spiritual disciplines, gratitude, and grace.

May you grow in patience, my friend, as you continue to inspire a joy for teaching and learning.

Love'em and Lead'em!

Active Question

Did I do my best to patiently persevere today?

SIMPLICITY IS A STRATEGY

Our life is frittered away by detail.
Simplify, simplify.

— HENRY DAVID THOREAU

In academia, the gravitational pull of complexity tends to overwhelm the opportunity to simplify.

After all, we're educators, right?

We have to prove our knowledge and expertise.

We don't have time to wait…

… and listen

… and perhaps admit we don't have all the answers.

Appearing to not know is way too vulnerable.

> *Nothing in all the world is more dangerous than*
> *sincere ignorance and conscientious stupidity.*
> — Martin Luther King, Jr.

The pitfalls of academic arrogance dangerously limit our influence and authenticity.

As we enter into a new season of learning and relationships, can we take a wiser approach? One that allows room for simplicity and humility?

We teach students that the key to solving math problems is to simplify because answers expressed in the simplest terms are the easiest to understand.

That works in education leadership as well.

> *Besides the noble art of getting things done, there is the noble art of leaving things undone.*
> *The wisdom of life consists in the elimination of non-essentials.*
> — Lin Yutang

One of our greatest contributions may be to simplify this work, enabling colleagues and students to focus on those core activities that make the greatest impact and allowing time to think deeply.

That requires us to …

    … Eliminate the non-essentials.

    … Confront dysfunctional habits.

    … Communicate key messages in consistent, disciplined ways.

That's how we inspire changes in behavior and motivate people to be their best.

Simplify the path for you and your people, maximizing the conditions for greater joy and growth.

Love'em and Lead'em!

WRITE THE NEXT CHAPTER

*There comes a point in your
life when you need to stop
reading other people's books
and write your own.*

– ALBERT EINSTEIN

All good things must come to an end--and that's especially true
after struggling through a challenging school year.

It's Over. Done. Finie.

Now what?

What will our narrative be next year?
How will we overcome the challenges and conquer the villains?

> *If you're not writing your own story,
> you're a character in someone else's.*
> – Chris Brogan

Be brave enough to be the author of your own story.

Don't let one difficult chapter define your whole life.

Learn from the previous chapters and determine to create an even better path forward.

Go deep on the stories of your life.

- What patterns do you see?
- Why did you make certain decisions?
- What did you learn about yourself?

Break down in detail what you love about each element and the feelings you experienced.

Self intelligence and awareness will help you create a more powerful narrative in this next chapter.

> *The stories we tell literally make the world.*
> *If you want to change the world, you need to change your*
> *story.*
> *This truth applies both to individuals and institutions.*
> — Michael Margolis

Great stories are simple and focused, with a very clear structure. So don't try to make it complicated. Focus on the small habits that build a pathway to success.

Finish this last chapter and move on so that you can get ready to do something even better!

Use your powerful story-building talents to create a new life-changing narrative through your courageous leadership as an educator.

Active Question

Did I do my best to live forward today?

PEACEMAKERS STANDOUT

Blessedness is promised to the peacemaker,
not to the conqueror.

— FRANCIS QUARLES

What is peace, my friend?
It's a word with lots of meaning:

Absence of conflict.
Unity.
Tranquility.
Agreement.
Public order.
State of mind.

(We host our annual "Gramps Camp" for one week each summer with lots of grandchildren at our house—we always have a blast, and yet the peace of silence is highly valued by the end 😃)

How does one become an effective peacemaker?

Practice, practice, practice.

> *People notice peacemakers because they dress funny. We know how the people who make war dress - in uniforms and medals, or in computers and clipboards, or in absoluteness, severity, greed, and cynicism. But the peacemaker is dressed in righteousness, justice, and faithfulness—dressed for the work that is to be done.*
> — Walter Brueggemann

Peace, like beauty, is largely based on perspective.

Parents, Students, Faculty, Administrators, Board Members, Donors—each and all have different views and versions of order and agreement.

They expect us as educators to wisely...

> ... keep the peace.
> ... make peace.
> ... hold our peace.

Peacemaking is a primary part of our job in order to sustain a healthy community. This includes resolving conflict by having the humility to genuinely listen, making adjustments rather than dogmatically defending the handbook, and creating a culture of follow-through that builds trust.

> *The weak can never forgive.*
> *Forgiveness is the attribute*
> *of the strong.*
> — Mahatma Gandhi

Forgiveness is a primary tool of the Peacemaker.

So is having the courage to vent to someone who will challenge our assumptions along with our willingness to hear them out.

Then, we can take the initiative to find a path to peace because when it comes to conflict, time doesn't heal--it usually enables the infection to spread.

Sharpen your tools as a peacemaker, my friend, to restore relationships and grow in grace.

Love'em and Lead'em!

Active Question

Did I do my best to make peace and resolve conflict today?

GRACEFUL GOODBYES

Some cause happiness wherever they go;
others whenever they go.

– OSCAR WILDE

The end of the school year is a time for goodbyes.

> Goodbye to some memories.
> Goodbye to some teachers and staff.
> Goodbye to graduates and some students.
> Goodbye to some families.

Did you know there are at least 41 ways to say goodbye in English?

Bye, Goodbye, See you, Good night, Have a good one, Bye-bye, Catch you later, Take care, Take it easy, Look after yourself, Ta-ta for now, So long, Farewell, See you next time, Don't be a stranger, Bye now, Talk soon, and the list goes on...

> *Great is the art of beginning,*
> *but greater is the art of ending.*
> – Henry Wadsworth Longfellow

How you end the year is as critical as how you begin it.

Too often we fail to intentionally plan how to end relationships, especially in the last weeks of the school year. People just move on and fade away, but that's not consistent with our mission.

We're trying to build long-term connections.

Experts trained in psychological therapies are equipped in the practice of termination, which occurs when they end a client relationship.

Breaking community can feel similar to mourning a death—sometimes, the emotional impact is similar.

When planned and executed properly, however, termination helps them leave the relationship with a healthy sense of closure and peace.

> *The story of life is quicker than the wink of an eye, the story of love is hello and goodbye, until we meet again.*
> – Jimi Hendrix

Often the best way for our people to renew their spirit is for us to listen to them reflect on their frustrations, fears, regrets, and wishes.

It takes energy and commitment to sustain engagement all the way to the end, but wise investments in saying goodbye and terminating relationships can be a powerful part of healing hearts and minds.

We're also laying the foundation for relationship renewal with faculty alumni, student alumni, and parent alumni, along with setting the tone for a healthy school culture next year.

May you experience joy in the endings, my friend, as you utilize your relational intelligence to bless and release.

Love'em and Lead'em!

Active Question

Did I do my best to foster healthy, long-term relationships today?

BEING CLEAN AND NEIGHBORLY

*Discretion will protect you, and
understanding will guard you.*

— PROVERBS 2:11

Everything was going as planned. We were packing for our up-
coming work with schools across various parts of Florida.
Halfway through washing my clothes, the dryer stopped working.

Are you kidding me?!
One load had just finished in the washer,
and the next one was ready.
Try as I might to "reboot" the dryer, it was committed to sit-
ting quietly still.

> *I believe you should live each day
> as if it is your last, which is why I
> don't have any clean laundry, because,
> come on, who wants to wash clothes
> on the last day of their life?*
> — Anonymous

165

I called the neighbor next door to see if I could dry the wet load in their dryer.

They moved in a few weeks earlier and kindly allowed me to bring my basket over.

It's such a blessing to have kind neighbors!

From my other pile of dirty clothes, I picked out the items I most needed and washed a small load.

Not wanting to impose on the neighbors again,

I decided to discreetly hang my clothes up in the backyard. I tried to find a place that had limited line of sight to the neighbors' windows, knowing they didn't want to see my *personables* hanging about.

> *Maybe a good rule in life*
> *is never become too important*
> *to do your own laundry.*
> — Barry Sanders

Transparency has consequences, and some things just need to be kept private. Wisdom is found in knowing the difference.

I began to realize advantages of the clothes dryer that are underestimated:

    privacy,
    convenience, and
    soft clothes, to name a few.

Fortunately, it was warm that day, and my clothes dried fairly quickly.

After a few hours, I gathered them up and went back to packing.

May you be blessed with kind neighbors, the wisdom of discretion, and clean laundry.

Love'em and Lead'em!

Active Question

Did I do my best to be a kind neighbor today?

FRIENDS MATTER

*Friendship is the hardest thing in the
world to explain. It's not something
you learn in school. But if you haven't
learned the meaning of friendship,
you really haven't learned anything.*

— MUHAMMAD ALI

My mom gave me a banner when I was about eight years old
that hung in my room for many years.

She placed it in a position so that I would frequently see it—
adjacent to the toilet in a tiny half-bath.

That banner had colorful smiley faces scattered across the can-
vas along with this poem about being friendly:

Begin the day with friendliness,
Keep friendly all day long

Keep in your heart a friendly song,
in your heart a happy song

Have in your mind a word of cheer
for all who come your way

And they will greet you, too, in turn, and wish you a happy day.

I read those verses every day, and it actually helped influence my attitude.

Repetition makes a difference, and being friendly has proven to be an asset in building relationships and achieving my goals.

Friends know the real you and still like you.

Friends overlook your messes and even help clean them up.

Friends celebrate good times and provide support during tough times.

Friends increase your sense of belonging and purpose.

Friends boost your happiness and confidence, encouraging you to be your best.

Friends listen to you and truly understand you.

> *A friend loves at all times, and*
> *a brother is born for adversity.*
> — Proverbs 17:17

A single friend can make a big difference in our life but can also be hard to find--especially with all of the stresses involved in education leadership.

We gain many benefits from intentional being and finding a friend, including not being lonely and isolated, less stress, and a sense of belonging.

Prioritize being a friend who is always ready with a smile and a word of cheer.

Love'em and Lead'em!

Active Question

Did I do my best to be a friend today?

FOR EXAMPLE

Example is not the main thing
in influencing others.
It is the only thing.

— ALBERT SCHWEITZER

Do you remember your teachers and other educators from your school days?

I can remember most of mine K-12 and from college. My sister can remember all of her teachers and most of mine. She's gifted that way.

Some we remember more fondly because of their life-changing example.

Who is an educator that made a significant impact on your life?

What adjectives or characteristics would you use to describe that person?

We ask that question often at faculty workshops and leadership retreats.

The answers almost always describe an educator who believed in them, pushed them to be their best with high expectations, and served as an example worth following.

Example is the school of mankind,
and they will learn at no other.
— Edmund Burke

The greatest asset of a school is the attitude of its educators.

It's a fact: The quality and attitude of the educators in a school matter most to student growth and development—way more than all other factors combined.

We model how to set aspirational goals and follow through on commitments.

We model how and when to take risks, going outside the comfort zone to grow.

We model perseverance and persistence, overcoming the barriers to find a way.

Without a doubt, the best way to love and lead peers and pupils is by example.

Because educators are remembered by hundreds and thousands of people!

In every way be an example of doing
good deeds. When you teach, do it
with honesty and seriousness.
— Titus 2:7

The influence of educators on the lives of students and others is exponential and can't really be measured because we engage their minds and their hearts.

174

They observe our actions, attitudes, and adaptations, learning both knowledge and practical skills that will forever shape their lives.

This is especially true during times of transition, like at the end of the school year when the pace of activities accelerates, relationships become more fragile, and the workload is unyielding. This is when our example is tested and refined the most.

Love'em and Lead'em!

Active Question

Did I do my best to make peace today?

UNCOMFORTABLE GROWTH

*Self-pity in its early stage is as snug
as a feather mattress. Only when it
hardens does it become uncomfortable.*

— MAYA ANGELOU

During an executive coaching session with Tom, he got to the heart of the problem:

We're going to have to get comfortable with being uncomfortable.

The leadership team was struggling a bit with implementing a culture of accountability with their core values. It's uncomfortable having those conversations and encouraging behavior change.

But those crucial conversations are unavoidable if we're going to become authentically excellent.

*God, make me so uncomfortable
that I will do the very thing I fear.*
— Ruby Dee

Every educator deals with strained relationships and hard situations, and the ones who are wise find a way to use these as opportunities to make themselves better.

One thing that can be really uncomfortable is telling people the truth, and giving direct feedback on issues that are negatively impacting the culture.

These may be hard things to share, but our integrity and leadership quality is weighed in the balance.

Are we willing to be uncomfortable?
To do the uncomfortable things?

Avoiding uncomfortable situations may offer temporary relief but usually creates long-term consequences. Complacency and procrastination undermine our goals.

> *For God gave us a spirit*
> *not of fear but of power*
> *and love and self-control.*
> — 2 Timothy 1:7

When we get comfortable with being uncomfortable, we may just discover a deeper strength--one that enables us to achieve an even higher level of success.

Moving beyond our comfort zone and proactively addressing the issues will accelerate our executive presence and ability to create excellence.

Try it. Sure it can be exhausting, but it's a small price to pay for making progress toward your dreams.

Push through with the uncomfortable but necessary, my friend, to grow in presence and progress.

Love'em and Lead'em!

Active Question

Did I do my best to do the uncomfortable things today?

THE BLAME GAME

*My lack of success
is self-imposed.*

— DENZEL WASHINGTON AS ROMAN J. ISRAEL, ESQ.

From the beginning, human nature has been predisposed toward blame. We can always find someone to blame—just like in Genesis, where Adam blamed Eve, and Eve blamed the snake.

We can …

… Blame our predecessor.
… Blame our boss.
… Blame our competition.

Blaming does have consequences, though.

People who blame others for their failures:

- Lose credibility as a leader
- Learn less about themselves and how to grow, and
- Lower their achievement compared to those who choose to own their errors and make adjustments accordingly.

Research shows that the same applies to organizations. Schools with a rampant culture of blame have a significant disadvantage when it comes to the capacity to grow, learn, and innovate.

Having a scapegoat draws attention away from the real and sometimes painful issues that still exist but are much harder to resolve.

We've seen this occasionally while working through the data analysis in a School Growth Plan—the leadership wasn't emotionally ready to face the truth, so they opted to play the blame game and avoid the hard conversations.

> *People are always blaming their circumstances for what they are. I don't believe in circumstances. The people who get on in this world are the people who get up and look for the circumstances they want, and if they can't find them, make them.*
> — George Bernard Shaw, in Mrs. Warren's Profession

Blaming is incredibly contagious, and it only prolongs the path of frustration and keeps our culture mired in dysfunction.

When we can accept that our problems are our own, we have the ability to control our own destiny.

No matter how frustrated, disappointed, and discouraged we may feel in the face of difficult situations, we can move beyond blame and resentment to courageously deal with the underlying issues with humility and grace.

To grow, we have to stop letting the past dominate our narrative and start creating a story of progress and success.

If we can sustain a culture where learning rather than blame is the priority, then we will maximize our influence and impact.

Such a shift in mindset advances our emotional intelligence, enabling us to respond with solutions that enable beauty and growth.

Lead forward, my friend, honoring and learning from the past with a radical commitment to healthy habits.

Love'em and Lead'em!

Active Question

Did I do my best to own mistakes and avoid blame today?

CONFLICT RESOLUTION

Peace is not absence of conflict, it is the
ability to handle conflict by peaceful means.

— RONALD REAGAN

A significant part of our work as an educator involves navigating conflict—some minor and some big ones—in a manner that sustains relationships and a healthy culture.

At the root of any such dispute is a difference in perspective. Our perceptions tend to be one-sided, and we can become quite emotionally attached to our biases.

To assess our ability to lead and love through conflict, consider these questions:

- Am I able to see each situation through the lens of that Teacher? Student? Parent? Administrator?
- Can I get beyond my assumptions, as difficult as that can be, to genuinely listen and seek to understand?
- Do I understand their pain and what they hope to gain?

The culture of our school, especially the community of relationships that we repeatedly tout, is directly impacted by our ability to hear and value their perspective.

Understanding others is knowledge,
Understanding oneself is enlightenment;
Conquering others is power,
Conquering oneself is strength.

— Laoz

We don't know what we don't know about them.

But we're not alone—everyone is constantly mired in profound ignorance when it comes to understanding other people—even those who may be very close.

Our calling and commitment to the noble profession of education requires daily recommitment to:

- **Unity of mind with humility**
  Agreement on everything is an elusive goal, but the power of unity can still prevail-- enabling teamwork and engagement to inspire learning. Begin with clarity on the mission and core values, and sustain it through the constant exercise of humility and consistent follow through.

- **Empathetically Listen**
  When we share the feelings of another, we only begin to understand their journey and who they are as a person. Sit and listen without trying to solve the problem or shift perspective. We can just be still and quiet in that dark place with them, ensuring they're not alone.

- Love with a tender heart

It's easy to get jaded in this work of education leadership. In a society so committed to react in outrage, we must remember that we're more concerned with people's hearts than making judgments or casting blame. Our leadership requires a deep love for people— throughout the campus!

Resolve conflict with unity, humility, and empathy because you're changing lives!

Love'em and Lead'em!

Active Question

Did I do my best to emphatically listen and love people today?

FOLLOW THROUGH

*People will follow you when you build
the character to follow through.*

--ORRIN WOODWARD

Our leadership influences the trajectory of people's lives.

They will give us a certain amount of respect just because of our title. If we fail to follow through, however, we lose that credibility rather quickly, and dysfunction prevails.

Follow through is a critical habit for leadership and for life. The value of our contribution depends on our ability to overcome an endless array of distractions and dysfunction to achieve our goals.

Those who are faithful, focused, and follow through are more effective and joyful.

*Good thoughts are no better than good
dreams if you don't follow through.*
— Ralph Waldo Emerson

Declaring plans and goals is easier than accomplishing them. The difficulty lies in the commitments made through the planning process and in the narrative created. Failing to follow through destroys trust--and that's hard to recover.

Be one of the faithful few who do.

If you say you're going to do something, do it on time and as promised.

That's more likely to happen if you start the day and end the day with a carefully planned ritual of reflection and preparation.

> *Whoever can be trusted with very little*
> *can also be trusted with much,*
> *and whoever is dishonest with very little*
> *will also be dishonest with much.*
> — Luke 16:10

Core to our leadership is creating the best conditions for talented people to thrive. We do that best through...

... remarkably clear expectations
... reliable communication and feedback,
... relentless following through.

Don't our students and families deserve educators who deliver results?

Even when our mind and body are urging us to postpone or even run from that difficult conversation or task, we muster the courage to follow through on what we believe and know is the right thing to do.

That's what sets courageous leaders like us apart from the rest.

We can use incentives and motivators to help us follow through, and even enlist a colleague or coach to keep us accountable to our commitments. Our legacy is worth it!

Love'em and Lead'em!

Active Question

Did I do my best to follow through today?

OVERCOMING FATIGUE AND FEAR

Fatigue makes cowards of us all ...
Endurance is relative to how
well the body is prepared.

— U.S. GENERAL GEORGE PATTON

When we're tired, we make more mistakes, we tend to compromise on what we know is the right thing to do, and our will to win is weaker.

Fatigue makes cowards of us all. A tired mind and body doesn't have the same resolve to lead, causing us to be more tempted to take the easy way out.

The school year sustains a relentlessly intense pace, with even the best becoming weary—especially during the spring months.

- It's the peak of the enrollment season for next year.

- Employment contract decisions are due soon.

- Difficult conversations with certain people need to happen.

- Discipline issues are increasing.

- Spring fever is at pandemic levels.

- Trying to keep up with the hectic schedule is exhausting.

We experience various types of fatigue: mental, emotional, spiritual, and physical. All with different symptoms and signs that can deceive some into making decisions out of fear.

> *Fear defeats more people than*
> *any other one thing in the world.*
> — Ralph Waldo Emerson

Fear is highly effective at weakening our leadership, killing relationships, and destroying dreams. How can we fend off the fears and fatigue to keep growing?

1. **Find a Mentor** who will hold us accountable to stay organized, disciplined, and focused--taking care of the little things produces big results.

2. **Fix the Process** instead of constantly being dominated by the tyranny of the urgent--our job is to make the more difficult decisions rather than so much of the routine stuff.

3. **Grow the Team** with consistently enforced expectations for collaboration and problem-solving—the benefits of a highly talented and engaged team are immeasurable.

A boat is safe in the harbor. But, this is not the purpose of a boat.

— Paulo Coelho

You have been blessed with incredible talents and opportunities to influence the lives of others, and your ability to navigate through the inevitable fatigue and fears will yield many rewards.

Lead with purpose, my friend, utilizing your self-intelligence to overcome the inevitable distractions and powerfully inspire others.

Love'em and Lead'em!

Active Question

Did I do my best to prepare my mind and body to maximize my performance today?

HAPPY THINKING

*Most folks are as happy as they
make up their minds to be.*

— ABRAHAM LINCOLN

"Happy Monday!" I said, walking down the hallway.

"Is it really happy?" my fellow educator asked. "Have you seen my to-do list?"

Finding joy is a habit that makes an impact—on our peers, our students, and everyone.
Remember Peter Pan? He had his happy thought, enabling him to fly and be free.

"Hook" is one of my favorite movies. Robin Williams and Julia Roberts did such an incredible job depicting Peter's rediscovery of his happy thought.

(One of my joy triggers is "Bangarang!")

> *The art of being happy lies in the*
> *power of extracting happiness*
> *from common things.*
> — Henry Ward Beecher

Joy can happen when we remember how good things really are.

Shouldn't every teacher and student have the privilege of experiencing joy at school? Isn't an attitude of joy core to our purpose as an educator?

A joyful school begins with you and me. We cannot cure all the ills of the world, but we can choose to live and learn in joy. Sometimes we need to pause in the busyness of our work and just be joyful.

Joy is a state of mind.
Joy is a state of grace.
Joy is a statement of heart.

> *The joy that isn't shared dies young.*
> — Anne Sexton

(Another one of my joy triggers is remembering my mother singing to me at a moment of severe grumpiness, "You can smile anytime, anywhere")

Joy is expressed in your face.

Sometimes your smile triggers a joyful spirit, and sometimes your joyful spirit emerges as a smile.

Joy is expressed in your response.

We know the obstacles are coming--embracing them enables you to reach that next level of joy.

Joy is expressed in your gratitude.

Joy shared is joy multiplied.

Joy is expressed in your encouragement.

Joy is an investment into the heart and soul of your people.

Joy is expressed in your empowerment.

Incredible joy comes from equipping and supporting others to achieve their goals.

Joy is expressed in your understanding.

One of the greatest expressions of love and joy is humbly and genuinely listening.

Give them some joy, my friend, keeping that happy thought so you can fly!

Love'em and Lead'em!

Active Question

Did I do my best to share joy today?

REGULAR REST

Don't underestimate the value of doing nothing,
of just going along, listening to all the things
you can't hear, and not bothering.

— A.A. MILNE

When your computer or anything electronic locks up, what's the first thing tech support tells you to do?

Reboot or unplug it for a few minutes to let the charge dissipate, then turn it back on. It's the universal first step to problem-solving.

Our bodies are similar. If we can unplug and relax for a few minutes every hour or so, we can actually become more productive.

Instead, we tend to blow through the stop signs and regret it later. The pace of life for us educators tends to be non-stop.

It's time to reframe what we know about stopping to do nothing.

Stop thinking of sleep and naps as 'downtime' or as a 'waste of time.' Think of them as opportunities for memory consolidation and enhancing the brain circuits that help skill learning. Nor should you feel guilty about sleep. It's just as crucial a part of successful brain work as the actual task itself.
— Richard Restak

Because of the frenetic schedule that is imposed on faculty and families, schools may be one of the biggest contributors to stress and unhealthy lifestyles. We cram as much as we can into a class period, give little time for changing classes or subjects, and keep that unrelenting schedule going throughout the day.

Could it be that naptime should be added to the daily schedule for the benefit of us all?

Intentionally stopping for a few minutes allows our minds to renew and revitalizes our bodies.

Educators, in general, tend to be sensitive people who engage their emotions throughout the day. We need time to retreat from the world in order to recuperate and recharge.

I've decided to be happy because it is good for my health.
— Voltaire

It must be okay to rest!
No matter how strong you think we are, we cannot live a stressful, maxed-out life without it eventually having consequences

202

on our minds and bodies. Is that really the model we want to be?

Who we are is so much more vital than what we do or what we know.

To maximize our valuable leadership, we need to set parameters, schedule breaks, and take care of ourselves--especially during breaks in the calendar.

Make the time to pause and rest—and then go the extra mile to exceed expectations. It's worth it to more fully enjoy life and fulfill your purpose.

Love'em and Lead'em!

Active Question

Did I do my best to allow time to rest my mind and spirit today?

LIVE RESPONSIVELY

It is wise to direct your anger towards problems—not people; to focus your energies on answers—not excuses.

— WILLIAM ARTHUR WARD

Why do bad things happen?

A 2021 Pew Research Center survey of Americans found that:

35% accepted that terrible experiences are an inevitable part of life
13% attributed human suffering to God's will
8% blamed sin and evil
8% viewed free will as the cause

A smaller percentage optimistically found that times of hardship provide opportunities for growth.

Our perspective on problems makes a difference.

Any answer to the question of why we suffer through difficult times is unsatisfying, and maybe that's because it's the wrong question.

> *Be grateful for what you have and stop complaining—it bores*
> *everybody else, does you no good, and doesn't*
> *solve any problems.*
> — Zig Ziglar

Perhaps the better question is:

> WHEN bad things happen, how do we respond so that
> we ultimately make the experience better for ourselves
> and those around us?

Painful times and situations are part of the journey of life.

We are more effective in our influence as educators when we not only accept that problems are going to happen but also develop the wisdom to expect them.

Education is solving problems--not just those on paper but throughout life.

Education is resolving conflict, restoring dignity and relationships.

Education is evolving with new solutions that enable us to adapt.

> *Do not be overcome by evil,*
> *but overcome evil with good.*
> —Romans 12:21

Victory in the midst of hardship doesn't come through complaining or giving up.

We win by confronting it courageously and choosing to live responsively. That requires a higher level of intelligence: Emotional, Spiritual, and Practical.

Through humility we choose to love and serve our colleagues and families, going above and beyond for those who may seek to discourage or defeat us.

We teach and lead with unusual enthusiasm and focus, resisting the temptation to engage in dishonorable behavior that would cause problems for others. We remain resolute in our mission because educators change lives!

Get ready for the problems that will certainly arise, responsively persevering to find the opportunities for joy hidden in the journey.

Love'em and Lead'em!

Active Question

Did I do my best to live responsively today?

ABOUT THE AUTHOR

Scott E. Barron is an educator, entrepreneur, and author recognized as a leading voice advocating for and mentoring educators in their calling and influence. He serves as the Chief Reinvention Officer of School Growth (SchoolGrowth.com) and the Executive Director of Educators Fellowship (EdFellowship.org).

He earned his M.Ed from Johns Hopkins University, along with a B.A. in Religion and a B.S. in Computer Science from Mars Hill University. His combination of experience as an educator, business leader, EdTech advisor, college instructor, author, and executive coach gives him a unique perspective to encourage and elevate those who educate.

May your journey as an educator be blessed!